SCOOBY-DOO! ™

UNMASKS MONSTERS

The Truth Behind Zombies, Werewolves, and Other Spooky Creatures

BY MARK WEAKLAND AND TERRY COLLINS
ILLUSTRATED BY CHRISTIAN CORNIA, DARIO BRIZUELA,
AND SCOTT NEELY

CAPSTONE YOUNG READERS
a capstone imprint

Published in 2015 by Capstone Young Readers,
A Capstone Imprint
1710 Roe Crest Drive
North Mankato, Minnesota 56003
www.capstoneyoungreaders.com

CAPS33845

**Cataloging-in-Publication information is on file with
the Library of Congress.**
ISBN 978-1-62370-216-8 (paperback)
Written by Mark Weakland and Terry Collins.

Editorial Credits:
Editor: Shelly Lyons
Designer: Ted Williams
Art Director: Nathan Gassman
Production Specialist: Tori Abraham

Design Elements:
Shutterstock: ailin1, AllAnd, hugolacasse, Studiojumpee

The illustrations in this book were created
traditionally, with digital coloring.

Thanks to our adviser for her expertise, research,
and advice: Elizabeth Tucker Gould, Professor of English
Binghamton University

Printed in China.
092014   008475RRDS15

MEET THE MYSTERY INC. GANG!

SCOOBY-DOO

SKILLS: Loyal; super snout

BIO: This happy-go-lucky hound avoids scary situations at all costs, but he'll do anything for a Scooby Snack!

SHAGGY ROGERS

SKILLS: Lucky; healthy appetite

BIO: This laid-back dude would rather look for grub than search for clues, but he usually finds both!

FRED JONES, JR.

SKILLS: Athletic; charming

BIO: He's the leader and oldest member of the gang. He's a good athelete and a good sport!

DAPHNE BLAKE

SKILLS: Intelligence; beauty

BIO: As a 16-year-old fashion queen, Daphne solves her mysteries in style.

VELMA DINKLEY

SKILLS: Clever; highly intelligent

BIO: Although she's the youngest member of Mystery Inc., Velma's an old pro at catching crooks.

MEET THE MONSTERS!

WEREWOLVES

SKILLS: Strength; super senses

BIO: These monsters are humans in the form of wolves. Legends say werewolves never die!

ZOMBIES

SKILLS: Super stinky; never tires

BIO: Zombies are known as the walking dead. They're hungry for human brains!

VAMPIRES

SKILLS: Strength; shape-shifting

BIO: Vampires are out for human blood! They're afraid of sunlight, and they always find ways to trick humans.

SEA MONSTERS

SKILLS: breathing fire; sneaking up on ships

BIO: These monsters of the deep can take many forms, but they're always super creepy!

MUMMIES

SKILLS: Strength; moving things with their minds

BIO: These moaning monsters take their sleep seriously and don't like being disturbed! They often carry a curse.

GHOSTS

SKILLS: Invisibility; noise-making

BIO: Although ghosts are often heard and not seen, they still find ways to creep out humans. They've even been known to move things!

TABLE OF CONTENTS

SCOOBY-DOO!

and the
Truth Behind
WEREWOLVES

Scooby-Doo and the gang were returning from a
walk in the park. Suddenly, Scooby-Doo perked up his ears.

"What's wrong, Scoob?" asked Shaggy.

"Rerewolf!" barked Scooby. "Up there!"

"Really?" asked Velma.

"Are you sure?" asked Fred. "Do you know what a werewolf is?"

"Maybe," said Daphne. "Stories say they live in houses and apartment buildings—just like humans. Werewolves are found all around the world."

"How do people become werewolves?" asked Shaggy.

"Legends tell us some people become werewolves through magic," said Velma.

"Others change when a werewolf bites them," added Fred. "Or when they drink water that a wolf has touched."

"When do werewolves change from human to wolf?" asked Shaggy.

"Only at night," said Fred.

"When the moon is full," said Daphne. "Like tonight. Look for a werewolf in the moonlight, and listen for its howling."

"Like, do werewolves have superpowers?" asked Shaggy.

"You bet," answered Daphne. "Legends say they are really strong."

"And don't forget about their senses," said Velma. "They have extraordinary vision, hearing, and sense of smell."

"Werewolves are vicious hunters," said Daphne.

"True," said Fred. "And once they taste blood, they crave it."

"Also, unless they die while in human form," said Velma, "werewolves are immortal."

"They rever die?" gasped Scooby. "Ruh, roh!"

"Rolfsrane?" asked Scooby.

"A plant with a beautiful purple flower," said Velma. "It's very poisonous. That's why people don't grow it in flowerbeds."

Time for a review. What looks human but can change into a flesh-hungry wolf under a full moon?" asked Fred.

YOW!

"Rerewolf!" shouted Scooby.
Fred looked at Shaggy and laughed.
"Boy is this burrito hot!" cried Shaggy.

SCOOBY-DOO!

and the Truth Behind ZOMBIES

"Has anyone found Scooby yet?" Velma asked.

"The kitchen is all clear!" Shaggy replied.

"He wasn't in the Mystery Machine," said Fred.

"I found him!" said Daphne.

"Scooby-Doo!" Velma scolded. "Why are you hiding in the sofa?"

"Rombies!" yelled Scooby.

"Zombies are nothing to fear," said Daphne. "You just need to know more about them."

Well, voodoo zombies are quite different from other legendary zombies. In voodoo, a *bokor*, or sorcerer, makes people zombies.

A *bokor* gives his zombies a poisonous powder. The powder makes them his slaves.

"Are all zombies made by magic?" Shaggy asked.

"In movies and stories, zombies are created in other ways too," Velma replied. "Chemicals and even zombie viruses can turn people into zombies."

"So, always cover your nose when you sneeze, Scoob," Shaggy joked.

Velma smiled. "No sneezing necessary. But a zombie's bite can infect you, and then you become one of the walking dead!"

"Not that we're planning on looking ... ," Shaggy began.

"Uh-uh!" Scooby agreed, shaking his head.

"... but where can we find a zombie?" Shaggy finished.

"Wherever you want to look," said Fred. "According to legends environment doesn't affect zombies. They can live anywhere."

"Zoinks! That makes it even harder to hide!" Shaggy said.

"If hiding is no good, can I outrun a zombie?" Shaggy asked hopefully.

"Yes, you can," Velma said. "Running away from a zombie is always the best response in movies. But remember, even though zombies are slow, they never get tired."

"Luckily, as their bodies decay, they fall apart," Fred added. "Zombies are often missing a foot or a leg. Still, don't take them lightly."

43

"Well, stories say that zombies eat fresh meat from any living creature," Daphne continued. "Birds, horses ... dogs."

"Ruh, roh!" Scooby exclaimed.

"And um, people," Fred finished. "Some zombies' favorite thing to eat is human brains."

"It looks like Shaggy and Scooby found a great hiding spot!" said Daphne.

"Well, Scooby and Shaggy always were fast learners," laughed Velma.

SCOOBY-DOO!

and the Truth Behind GHOSTS

"Like, whose idea was it to spend the night in Baron Creepy's house again?" Shaggy asked.

"Act cool, team," said Fred. "The TV producers of *Ghost Grabbers* asked for us specifically."

"That's what worries me," Shaggy whispered.

"Shh!" Daphne hissed. "My microphone is picking up a spooky sound!"

"I'll tape it with the recorder," Velma said. "Fred, can you get closer with the video camera?"

"Where is Scooby?" Shaggy asked. "Oh, no! The ghost must have grabbed him!"

"The sound is coming from that suit of armor," Velma said.

As the gang watched, the visor of the helmet flipped open to reveal the face of Scooby-Doo!

"Boo!" barked Scooby.

Velma played back the recording. "GRRROWL!"

"Hey, that's not a ghost!" Daphne cried. "That's Scooby's stomach growling!"

"Like, who says ghosts really exist anyway?" asked Shaggy.

"Scientists say there are no ghosts, because there's no proof," Velma said. "But witnesses say otherwise."

"That's right," Fred added. "Paranormal investigators have heard strange sounds. They've also taken photos and videos that can't be explained."

"So, do ghosts exist or not?" Shaggy asked.

"It depends on whom you ask," replied Velma.

"And if ghosts are real, then what are they made of?" Shaggy asked.

"Ghosts often appear as a 'fog' called ectoplasm," Fred said.

"Other ghosts appear as a moving shadow. Sometimes they're even invisible!" Daphne added.

"Invisible?" Shaggy said.

Daphne nodded. "Some invisible ghosts make strange noises and knock pictures off of walls. They can even make a room feel cold."

They also can be found at places where they died, such as battlefields, prisons, or hospitals. And some ghosts hang around cemeteries.

"Zoinks! Run, Scoob!" Shaggy cried.

"Relax, Shaggy," Daphne said. "That's just your helmet light reflecting in the mirror."

"It looked like a ghost orb," Velma offered.

"What's a ghost orb?" Shaggy asked.

"It's a ball of light that often mysteriously appears in pictures," Fred answered. "Some people think these orbs might be ghostly spirits."

"Most orbs are really a camera's flash reflecting off dust particles in the air," Velma said. "But eyewitnesses have reported seeing orbs when the photos were taken."

Just us!" Shaggy replied, "We ran into the china cabinet."

"I thought the noise might have been a poltergeist," Velma said.

"What's a poltergeist?" Shaggy asked.

"It's a ghost that's heard but not seen. They make loud noises and hide things like a person's keys, " said Fred. "Sometimes an angry poltergeist even breaks dishes or other items."

"Remind me to stay away from poltergeists," Shaggy muttered.

"Reah!" Scooby agreed.

"Do ghosts haunt ships too?" Shaggy asked.

"Sure, the *Flying Dutchman* is thought to be a cursed ghost ship," Daphne replied.

"Rying Rutchman?" Scooby barked.

"It sails the world, haunting sailors in the black of night," Daphne explained.

"The *Flying Dutchman*'s crew of spirits is doomed to roam the oceans forever," Velma added. "According to legend seeing the ship is considered bad luck."

"Maybe we should stick to ghost hunting on dry land," Shaggy suggested.

"Do we have everything needed to find a ghost?" Shaggy asked.

"People use lots of different tools to find a ghost," Velma added. "We have the basics with us, but there are many useful tools."

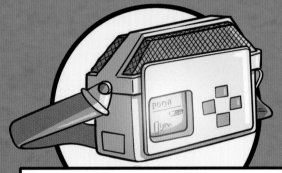

DIGITAL AUDIO RECORDER AND MICROPHONES

DIGITAL VIDEO CAMERA

DIGITAL STILL CAMERA WITH INFRARED CAPABILITIES

NIGHT VISION GOGGLES

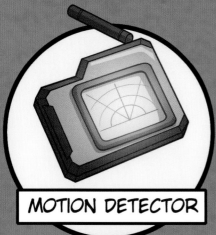

MOTION DETECTOR

ELECTROMAGNETIC FIELD (EMF) METER

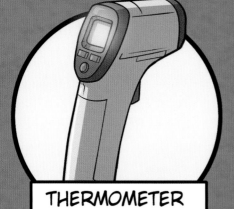

THERMOMETER

"Are there any ghosts of famous people?" Shaggy asked.

"Of course," Fred replied. "The ghost of the famous musician Elvis Presley is said to haunt Graceland. Graceland was his mansion in Memphis, Tennessee."

"Visitors to the White House say they have seen the ghost of former U.S. president Abraham Lincoln walking the halls," Daphne said.

"Like, if I saw one of those ghosts, I wouldn't know whether to run or ask for an autograph!" Shaggy joked.

So much for our television debut," Shaggy said. "We're back where we started from and still no ghosts!"

"Oh, I wouldn't say that," Fred said. "Check behind you."

"Raggy!" Scooby said. "Rook!"

"H-h-haunted knight!" Shaggy cried. "Gangway!"

"Oh, well. *Ghost Grabbers* can always use this footage for a comedy," Daphne laughed.

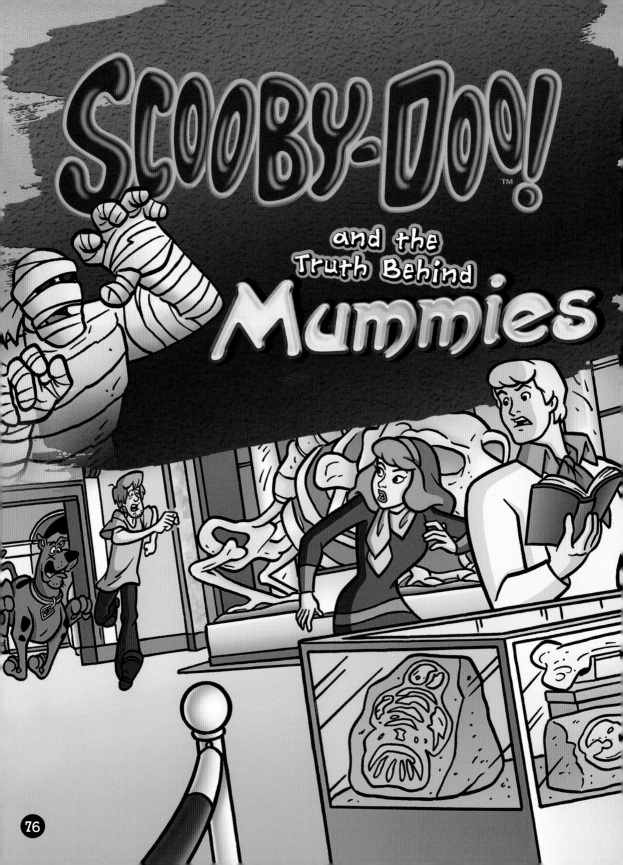

SCOOBY-DOO!™

and the
Truth Behind
Mummies

Scooby-Doo and the gang were visiting the museum. They were excited to see the new exhibits. But Scooby and Shaggy were nowhere to be found.

"This museum is so big," said Velma. "I hope they didn't get lost."

The quiet was broken when Shaggy and Scooby burst into the room. "Rummy!" barked Scooby.

"He thinks he saw a mummy!" yelped Shaggy. "In the Ancient Egypt room!"

"A human body," said Fred. "Ancient Egyptians removed the brain and other internal organs. They left the heart in place. Then the body was dried with a salt called natron and wrapped in linen."

"Why?" asked Scooby.

"To prepare it for the afterlife," said Velma.

"The brains were removed too," added Daphne. "But in stories or movies, mummies are smart, even without brains."

"Then the body was placed in a coffin. Sometimes the coffin was placed into a stone coffin called a sarcophagus," said Velma. "Then the sarcophagus was put into a tomb."

"How do we know if a mummy is chasing us?" asked Shaggy nervously.

"In movies mummies often moan," said Fred. "And shuffle their feet."

"Roaning and ruffling?" Scooby said.
"And a mummy is wrapped in cloth,"
said Velma. "That's a dead giveaway!"

"Yes," said Fred. "In movies and stories, mummies are very strong. And they carry a curse that affects those who disturb them. Sometimes they have special powers too."

"Some can move objects just by thinking. That's called telekinesis," said Velma.

"And some control insects, wind, or sand with their minds," added Daphne.

"Bugs!" yelled Shaggy.

"Yuck!" barked Scooby.

PIZZA

"You don't have to worry," said Daphne. "Legendary mummies are strong, but they move slowly.

"Another way to protect yourself is with fire," said Fred. "Mummies catch fire easily because of their wrappings. If you set one on fire, it will be destroyed."

"Rokay!" said Scooby.

SCOOBY-DOO!™
and the Truth Behind
SEA MONSTERS

The weather at the beach was beautiful. Velma opened the picnic cooler. "Lunch time, gang!" she yelled. "Hey, where's Scooby?"

"No sign of him here!" Shaggy replied.

"He's not on the beach," Fred said.

"Scooby-Doo, where are you?" Daphne called toward the ocean.

"Rover here!" Scooby cried.

"Like, you totally crushed my castle, Scoob," said Shaggy. Scooby pointed toward the water. "Rea ronster!" he yelled.

"So how big do sea monsters get, anyway?" Shaggy wondered.

"Well, the Leviathan was one of the biggest sea creatures of legend," said Fred. "One report had him being 900 miles (1,448 kilometers) long!"

"I'm sorry I asked," Shaggy said.

"He had rows of sharp teeth," Fred continued, "and breathed fire."

"Yikes!" said Scooby.

"So what's the most famous sea monster?" Shaggy asked.

"That's easy," replied Daphne. "The Loch Ness monster, or Nessie."

"Ressie?" asked Scooby.

Nessie has a small head and a long neck. She also has at least one hump on her back. Tourists from all around the world travel to Loch Ness in Scotland to try and see her. But Nessie has never been caught. Some people think she's a myth.

"So, have sea monsters ever attacked people?" Shaggy asked.

"Some of them, yes," Velma replied. "The mythical kraken was probably based on the real giant squid that still live today. The kraken lived off the coasts of Norway and Greenland. It grew up to 50 feet (15 m) long."

"Rig rea ronster!" Scooby said.

"Very big," said Fred. "With eight long arms, it was said to easily grab ships and pull them under water."

"Yes," said Velma. "It lives in and around the Congo River in Africa."

"No one has ever gotten a picture or any proof of the monster," Fred added. "But experts think it could be a long-lost dinosaur."

"It's said to have the body of an elephant and a long, flexible neck and tail," said Velma.

"According to the crew of the *Kuranda*, yes!" Velma said. "In 1973 a giant jellyfish got stuck to the front of their ship."

"How big was it?" Shaggy wondered.

"It weighed about 20 tons (18 metric tons)," said Velma, as she showed the gang the screen. "The tentacles were more than 200 feet (61 m) long."

"What should I do if I see a sea monster?" Shaggy asked.

"If you can, take pictures or video of what you see," Daphne replied.

"Yes," said Fred, "and try to get a good shot. The pictures people have taken of the Loch Ness monster are blurry and dark."

SCOOBY-DOO!

and the Truth Behind
VAMPIRES

THE MYSTERY MACHINE

Daphne, Fred, and Velma were working late. It was time for a snack.

"Let's order a pizza," said Daphne.

"Speaking of pizza, I wonder where Scooby and Shaggy are?" said Fred.

Just then the phone rang. Shaggy was on the line. "Scoob thinks he saw a—"

"Rampire!" barked Scooby.

"That's right, a vampire at the corner of 4th and Main Street," said Shaggy.

"We're on our way!" said Velma.

124

Like, how do people become vampires?" asked Shaggy.

"In legends some people are born a vampire," said Daphne.

"But the most common way of becoming a vampire is to get bitten by one," said Fred.

"Ret's get out of here!" said Scooby.

So, if a vampire chases me, how do I escape?" asked Shaggy.

"Carry a bag of rice with you," said Fred. "If you're chased, spill the rice on the ground. A vampire will stop and count each grain!"

"Really?" asked Scooby.

"Bird seed works too," said Velma.

Like, where do vampires stay?" asked Shaggy.

"In houses and apartments," said Daphne.

"If they're rich they live in mansions and castles!" added Velma.

"During the day they sleep in coffins," said Fred.

Shaggy looked around nervously. "Do vampires have special powers?"

"Special powers?" asked Velma. "Yes. They have unnatural strength."

"And they can hypnotize you with their eyes!" said Fred.

"They can shape-shift too," said Daphne. "They turn into bats, rats, mist, and wolves!"

"Rikes!" said Scooby.

"What are vampires afraid of?" asked Shaggy.

"Many things," said Velma. "Sunlight and running water."

"Fire too!" exclaimed Daphne.

"And crosses," added Fred, "especially silver ones."

"Legends say they're most afraid of a wooden stake through the heart," said Velma. "A stake means the end for a vampire."

GLOSSARY

ancient—from a long time ago

canine teeth—long, pointed teeth that help people tear food

chemical—a substance that creates a reaction

coffin—a long container into which a dead person is placed for burial

curse—an evil spell meant to harm someone

decay—to break down into tiny pieces after dying

ectoplasm—a "fog" said to produce a spirit

electronic voice phenomena (EVP)—sounds heard on recordings that were not heard when originally recorded; some say EVP is the sound of ghosts

flesh—the soft part of an animal's body that covers the bones

hypnotize—to put a person into a sleeplike state

immortal—able to live forever

infect—to cause disease by introducing germs or viruses

internal organs—parts of the inside of the body; the heart, lungs, liver, and kidneys are organs

linen—cloth made from a flax plant

legend—a story passed down through the years that may not be completely true

myth—a story told by people in ancient times; myths often tried to explain natural events

mythical—imaginary or possibly not real

paranormal investigator—someone who studies events that science can't explain

poltergeist—a noisy ghost that sometimes moves, hides, or breaks things

shape-shift—to change physical form at will

squid—a sea animal with a long, soft body and 10 fingerlike arms to grasp food

telekinesis—power to move things with the mind

tentacle—a long, flexible limb used for moving, feeling, and grabbing

tomb—a room or building that holds a dead body

transform—to change form

venom—a poisonous liquid produced by some animals

vicious—fierce or dangerous

virus—a germ that infects living things and causes disease

INDEX

ABOUT THE AUTHORS

MARK WEAKLAND

Mark Weakland wears many hats. As an author, he's written books for teachers, including *Super Core!: Turbocharging Your Basal Reading Program with More Reading, Writing, and Word Work*, published by the International Reading Association. His book topics for children include sports, bacteria, comets, and poetry. Mark's also a reading specialist. He teaches kindergarten children, third graders, parents, and teachers.

As a musician and songwriter, Mark sings, plays percussion, and strums the guitar. Many of his songs, including *"I Sure Love Pancakes"* and *"The Dooflicky Machine,"* have won national awards and contests. Mark lives in Western Pennsylvania.

TERRY COLLINS

An award-winning newspaper reporter and columnist, Terry Collins now writes fiction, nonfiction, poetry, and graphic novels for readers of all ages. Some of his latest titles include biographies of Elvis Presley and Louis Armstrong, a historical fiction novel of Ancient China, and a graphic novel on the unsung heroes of World War II.

A National Board Certified English instructor, he now teaches literature and creative writing in his hometown of Mount Airy, North Carolina. Despite a lack of shelf space for his ever-growing library, he will always believe a person can never have too many books.

ABOUT THE ILLUSTRATORS

CHRISTIAN CORNIA

Christian Cornia was born in Modena, Italy on September 8, 1975. From 1996–1997 he attended the school of comics, La Nuova Eloisa, in Bologna, Italy.

He has created artwork and characters for several publishers, advertisers, video games, and role-playing games, and has worked as a colorist for French publishers such as Soleil, Delcourt, and Dargaud. Christian has also worked as an inker for Marvel Comics on such titles as *Marvel Adventures: Ironman*; *Marvel Adventures: Avengers*; and *Daken: Dark Wolverine*.

In 2011 Christian joined other italian artists in the cultural association Dr. INK, which self-produces illustration books. Christian currently works as an artist on Scooby-Doo for Italian publisher Piemme Edizioni, and teaches character design at the International School of Comics in Reggio Emilia, Italy.

DARIO BRIZUELA

Dario Brizuela was born in Buenos Aires, Argentina, and as a teen he began studying at an art school—doing drawing, sculpture, painting, and more. After discovering superhero comic books, his goal was to draw his favorite characters.

He broke into comics by working for publishers such as Dark Horse Comics; Image; Mirage Studios; IDW; Titan Publishing; Soleil Productions; Viz Media; Little, Brown and Company; DC Comics; and Marvel Comics; and for companies like Hasbro and Lego. His comic book and illustration work in the United States and Europe includes: *Star Wars Tales*, *Dioramas, Ben 10, Super Friends, Justice League Unlimited, Voltron Force, Batman: The Brave and the Bold, Transfomers, Mini Hulks, Gormiti, Superhero Squad, Scooby-Doo,* and *Beware the Batman*.

SCOTT NEELY

Scott Neely has been a professional illustrator and designer for many years. Since 1999 he's been an official Scooby-Doo and Cartoon Network artist, working on such licensed properties as *Dexter's Laboratory, Johnny Bravo, Courage The Cowardly Dog, Powerpuff Girls,* and more. He has also worked on *Pokémon, Mickey Mouse Clubhouse, My Friends Tigger & Pooh, Handy Manny, Strawberry Shortcake, Bratz,* and many other popular characters.

He lives in a suburb of Philadelphia and has a scrappy Yorkshire Terrier, Alfie.